OLIVER FRANKLIN

Animal Facts For Kids

100 Cool Facts About Your Favorite Animals

Contents

1

Introduction

Hello! If you are reading this book it is probably because you enjoy animals, and learning about them, as much as I do! Animals are awesome, and there are so many. From animals we might see more often like dogs, cats, cows, and horses, all the way to animals most of us might only see in a zoo, like lions, emus, and kangaroos. There are cool things to know about every one of the awesome animals we share the world with, and this book is going to share some facts about them so that we can keep having fun learning more about our furry, scaly, hairy, feathered, and shelled friends. This book is for the kid who wants to learn more about animals alone, or for a kid and an adult who want to read and learn together. Do whatever feels good for you, your reading level, and your happiness.

Why do I like animals so much? Great question! First off, they are awesome and I have enjoyed learning things about them my entire life. Also, I have been lucky enough to work and volunteer at several different animal sanctuaries all across the United States. I have worked up close with animals like wolves, horses, pigs, goats, tigers, lions, bears, bobcats, cheetahs, chimpanzees, and one very loud and hungry hyena named Helena. These adventures have made me even more curious and excited to learn more about not only these animals, but many more.

You should know, this book is not meant to teach you everything you need to know about all these animals. This book is my way of sharing some fun knowledge and encouraging other people to keep enjoying our animal friends. Some facts will be things I learned myself through my animal experiences, and some will be ones I am learning at the same time as you as I write this book. I may even include facts about individual animals if they are one I've worked with, like Hercules the chimpanzee or Rowdy the bear. Some facts will be cool, some will be fascinating, and some will be flat out silly, like how horses fart a lot. I'm glad we get to learn these things together and I am excited to see which facts end up being my favorite and your favorite. I hope your favorite animal is included, but if it isn't then I hope you learn a fact that gives you another animal to become a big fan of as well. If a certain fact catches your eye and you want to learn more, I encourage you to look it up and keep on learning.

So please enjoy, and make sure to call someone when you finish reading and tell them your favorite new fact!

Let's get started!

2

Farm Animals and Pets Introduction

These are animals that we usually think of as being pets or living on a farm, but that doesn't mean that they aren't also in the wild. In fact, almost all pets started as wild animals and humans tamed them. A lot of us have seen most of these animals in person, but that doesn't mean we know all these facts about them. Let's see what we can learn!

3

Dogs

There are over 350 different breeds of dogs. Believe it or not, that number is still growing too. Humans like to combine different breeds together to create dogs that might look or act in certain ways.

Like how humans can be right or left handed, dogs can be right or left pawed. You can often figure out if a dog is right or left pawed by which paw they step with first when they start to walk. They often prefer to use one side more often.

A dog's sense of smell is around 40 times better than a human's. Imagine how good some things could smell if we had a nose that powerful, or how bad other things could smell. It's no wonder now why dogs spend so much time smelling everything.

*I used to take care of a dog named Dukes, who loved to escape so that he could go swim in a pond. He never ran away or got lost. He just always ran to the pond.

4

Horses

Horses can sleep standing up or laying down. They get their deepest sleep when they lay down, but more often they take naps during the day while they are still standing up. You can often tell if a horse is napping or about to nap if one of their back legs is bent a little bit. They do that so that they can more easily lean to one side and be more comfortable and relaxed.

Horses cannot burp! It's true! But they make up for it by farting an awful lot.

Horses are group animals and like to live in herds. Like many animals, they have friends and even best friends, and will remember their friends and be happy to see them even if they haven't seen one another in years.

*My favorite horse was named Billy Bob, and he liked to lift me off the ground using just his head!

5

Pigs

Pigs are smart and good at many different puzzles. In fact, sometimes they can even open up the locks on their gates and escape from their pig pens. Trust me, they are great at that.

There are around 2 billion pigs on the planet and almost 8 billion humans! Who do you think would win in a mud bath competition?

Pigs build nests. They like to gather sticks, leaves, or whatever they have where they live, and make a soft and comfortable spot to relax.

The smallest pigs, Teacup pigs, can be as small as 50 pounds. That's very small considering that most pigs get to be between 300 and 700 pounds, and the world record for largest big was 2,252 pounds!

*I knew a pig named Petunia. Her back legs did not work, but she was still the fastest pig I've known because she learned to pull herself with her front legs. She was especially fast when we were bringing pig food.

6

Goats

Goats have 4 stomachs! They eat things like grass and hay, and having multiple stomachs helps them to digest their food.

Most of us are only used to seeing a few different kinds of

goats at farms and zoos, but there are actually over 200 kinds of goats in the world!

Goats were the first animal used by humans for milk. Goat milk is still popular in many places where there are not as many cows or other animals that make milk.

*Whenever I was cleaning the barn for a group of seven goats, I had to keep track of where one particular goat was. She was smaller than the rest of the goats and she loved to climb up high where the others couldn't get to and then wait to pounce on them, or me, as we walked underneath her. I nicknamed her "Ninja Goat."

7

Hamsters

Hamsters rely strongly on their hearing and sense of smell. Their eyesight is actually pretty bad. They are colorblind and nearsighted.

13

Hamsters have pouches in their cheeks that they can actually use to store food for later! What sort of food would you store for later if you could?

Hamsters are mostly nocturnal, and prefer to be active at night. That's why you have dreams about hamster wheels when you sleep in the same room as your little friend.

8

Goldfish

Goldfish don't have stomachs! It's best for them to have lots of small meals throughout the day instead of big meals because they don't have a stomach to help process the food.

Goldfish sleep with their eyes open because they do not have eyelids like we do. However, goldfish can actually see more colors than humans can. It makes me wish they could paint what they see.

It is possible for a goldfish to live over 40 years! When it comes to popular pets, goldfish can actually be one of the longest living ones. Their memories are also far better than people used to think, so even an old goldfish could tell you about its childhood full of swimming stories. Of course, if your goldfish CAN tell you that, please let me know because I would love to meet a talking goldfish.

9

Cats

H ousecats can jump 8 feet in the air! If they were human they could dunk a basketball easily.

Most cats spend 13 to 18 hours a day sleeping. There is a reason they call them "cat naps."

A lot of cats, from domestic cats to tigers, are fascinated by the smell of cinnamon and vanilla.

Housecats have retractable claws that let them choose when their claws come out. They'll bring them out to grab hold of things like prey, toys, or things they are climbing and don't want to fall off of.

*A cat named Toby used to climb to a platform above me and massage my head every time I brought him food. If I was wearing a hat he would grab it and toss it away first.

10

Parrots

Parrots are some of the smartest birds. They are able to figure out lots of different kinds of puzzles, memorize people's faces, and are even able to mimic the sounds of humans they spend time with by repeating words like "Hello."

There are many varieties of parrots. Most of them eat mainly seeds, but others also eat fruits, flowers, and small bugs. Their beaks are very strong and they can use them to crack and eat all sorts of crunchy things.

Parrots live longer than most animals that people can have as pets. Even longer than goldfish. Some parrots can live to be 80 years old!

11

Guinea Pigs

When Guinea pigs are happy or excited they make a high pitched squeak. They may even jump off the ground, which is called popcorning. This very often means they believe there is a good chance they are about to get food. Guinea pigs are even able to purr when being held, like a cat.

Guinea pig teeth never stop growing! Through eating and chewing things, the guinea pigs keep their teeth from getting too long.

When guinea pigs eat too quickly they can get hiccups.

Guinea pigs are thought to be a good pet for younger kids because they usually don't need much special care and can have relatively long and healthy lives compared to many small pets.

12

Chickens

When chickens get older, they lay fewer, but bigger eggs. A healthy chicken can lay around 265 eggs every year.

Chickens will sometimes eat gravel and dirt on purpose to help them digest other foods.

There are around 26 billion chickens in the world. That's more than any other kind of bird, and also means that there are around 2.3 chickens for every 1 human on Earth. Imagine the biggest room you have ever seen filled up with chickens.

Even though people call each other "chicken" to mean scared, chickens can actually be very brave when it comes to defending their baby chicks. They will fight off larger birds like hawks and eagles, and even snakes, that try to take their chicks.

13

Wild Animals Introduction

These animals are not pets, or at least shouldn't be! There are so many great wild animals to learn about, but this section will probably have a few of my personal favorites and ones that I have worked with.

14

Wolves

You can hear a wolf howl from 10 miles away. One of the reasons they howl at the full moon so much is because they like to howl before their pack goes hunting, and they like to hunt when there is a full moon because it gives them more light to see.

A wolf pack is very structured and every member has a role. The alpha wolves, the leaders, might make decisions about where the pack travels and when they hunt, and the omega wolves, or lowest ranking, help keep the pack happy by playing with everyone.

Wolves have partially webbed toes. This helps them be great diggers and swimmers!

*My favorite animal ever was a wolf named Isabeau. After she was done digging in the dirt she liked to step into a pool of water and make more digging motions to clean her paws. She would keep going until she was very wet, but very clean.

15

Frogs

F rogs don't drink water with their mouths. They have special patches of skin on their bellies and thighs that absorb water.

Frogs can jump 20 times their body length! Imagine if there were 20 of YOU laying down head to toe and you were able to jump over all of them.

Frogs actually do have ears. They are small, flat, and shaped like dinner plates. They are right behind a frog's eyes.

16

Chimpanzees

Chimpanzees are not monkeys. They are apes, and in fact they are 1 of 5 great ape species that include chimps, orangutans, gorillas, bonobos, and humans. One of the differences is that great apes do not have tails like most monkeys do.

Chimpanzees will groom each other to show friendship and to bond. They use their hands or sticks to clean dirt and bugs out of each other's hair.

Even though they can be very strong, chimpanzee bodies can get tired faster than ours. They can run faster and jump higher than we can, but we can do it for longer. However, don't challenge a chimp to a contest to see who can hang from a pull-up bar or tree branch the longest, because they can do that happily for hours.

MOST chimpanzees do not actually throw poop like they are often shown doing in cartoons. But many of them spit! They will spit at each other, and humans, sometimes as play and sometimes as an insult or to say they do not like something.

*I helped take care of a chimpanzee named Hercules who loved to show off and dance. Sometimes he challenged me to dance competitions. He would do a dance move from his side of the fence and then wait for me to do one, and then he would do another more crazy one, and we would take turns like that until he was confident he had won.

17

Orcas

Orcas have a couple of popular nicknames, like killer whales or "wolves of the sea." They get these names because they are very good hunters who are often able to get their prey. Also, just like wolves live in groups called packs, orcas live in groups called pods, and will hunt together as a team.

Their color pattern is to help them sneak up on their prey. Their white bellies help blend in with the bright sky when they are seen from below, and their black backs help them blend into the darkness of the deep ocean when they are seen from above.

Orcas are spread across the world, and can be found in every ocean. They often spend the year moving around as the weather changes, so that they can stay in their favorite temperatures.

Orcas aren't always being serious. Like with dolphins, orcas have been seen dancing, playing, and singing together to improve the bonds in their pods.

18

Tigers

A tiger's roar is so deep that humans can only hear about half of the sound, but we can feel the whole thing, which often makes people who have been around a roaring tiger call it one of the most powerful feeling animal sounds in the world. It sort of feels like your whole body is vibrating.

Every tiger has unique stripes! No two tigers will ever have the same pattern.

While most types of cats don't like to swim, tigers actually love it, and are very strong swimmers. They will go into water to clean themselves, cool off, and will sometimes even hunt in shallow water.

*Even though tigers in the wild usually live alone, except for a mother and cubs, I know two tigers named Duna and Elle Mae who have a very hard time falling asleep unless they are touching and snuggling with each other.

19

Giraffes

Giraffes are the tallest mammal on Earth, and can be almost 20 feet tall. That's the top of a basketball hoop that is sitting on top of a basketball hoop!

They almost never lay down. They spend almost all of their time standing, even when they sleep.

Giraffes have large black tongues that are extra tough. They use them to eat leaves from the tops of spiky trees without getting hurt. Their tongues are so long they can even use it to clean the inside of their ears!

Giraffes give birth while standing up. So the first thing a giraffe has to do in its life is try to land well.

20

Penguins

When they can, penguins move around on land by waddling or sliding on their bellies to save energy. Even though they may move on land in a way that can look silly, they are impressive swimmers. Once they get to the water they are very graceful and fast and can even dive to almost 6,000 feet!

Penguins have wings, but cannot fly. Their wings have special feathers that help them stay warm, camouflage, and change direction quickly when they are swimming.

Penguins bond for life, meaning that when they find a mate to have baby penguins with, they will spend the rest of their lives with them. Bonded penguins have been known to bring each other pebbles and other small things as gifts.

After a penguin lays an egg, the parents will take turns standing over it to protect it and keep it warm while the other one goes to get food.

21

Flamingos

Flamingos get their pinkish color from their diet. They are born white, but they eat so many pink plankton and shrimp that their feathers start getting that color. Don't worry, that doesn't happen to humans. Though if we could change our color by eating certain foods, what would you eat a lot of?

Flamingos often stand on one leg, but no one has been able to figure out why. The best guess is that because their legs do not have feathers, keeping them close to the rest of the body helps the legs stay warm.

Flamingos only lay one egg every year. Young flamingos usually stay close to their parents until the new chick is born.

Octopus

Most varieties of octopus can change their color to match their background, like a chameleon. They use this ability to ambush their prey. Their tentacles help them catch and hold their food and have small but powerful beaks to break their prey's shells.

An octopus can fit into tiny spaces! As long as a space or a whole is big enough for its hard beak, the rest of an octopus body is so flexible and squishable that it can fit through. This makes them great at hiding.

They can swim backwards very fast by shooting out a jet of water that helps push them back. They can do this if they accidentally bump into a predator.

Octopus can make themselves a shell out of things they find in the water. There are videos of them using things like open coconuts or glass jars that fell into the water as a makeshift shell and shelter.

23

Raccoons

Raccoons will eat almost anything, from fruits and vegetables to bugs and small lizards or snakes. Most raccoons we see near people's garbage cans won't get to be that big, but a raccoon with a healthy diet can get to be up to 60 pounds!

Raccoons always make sure to live close to water, and like to make their nests in hollow logs, tree trunks, or in small caves and burrows near rivers or ponds.

Often, a raccoon will dip its food in water before eating it. It does not seem like they are cleaning it, and scientists actually think that it may just be because they like the taste!

24

Baby Animals Introduction

Who doesn't love a baby animal? This section will look at animals specifically when they are babies or still very young. The facts might be about how they are born, how they grow up, or just how cool they are.

25

Black Bears

E ven though we think of bears as very large animals, black bears are less than 1 pound when they are born!

Bear cubs love to wrestle and play by fighting with their siblings, and can sometimes get very rough. They will keep going until their mother physically separates them.

Even as cubs, black bears are excellent tree climbers, and cubs will climb all the way to the tops of tall trees when they get scared.

*I once spent months living next to a black bear named Rowdy. His enclosure was outside of my kitchen window. He had a hammock that he loved to take naps in, and every morning when I was getting my food ready in the kitchen he would wake up and sit in his hammock and watch me make food. I'm pretty sure he always wanted me to share.

26

Rabbits

Baby Rabbits are called Kits or Kittens. A mother rabbit usually has 3-to 8 kits in a litter.

Wild rabbits are often born underground in dens and tunnels that their parents have dug. Sometimes it can take them weeks to go above ground for the first time.

A baby rabbit only needs to get milk from its mother once a day. The milk is so nutritious that one feeding a day is enough to help them grow.

27

Blue Whales

B lue whales are the largest babies in the world! When they are born they can already be 26 feet long and weigh almost

9 thousand pounds. That is already almost as heavy as a full grown African elephant.

A blue whale only has one baby at a time, and can have a baby every 3 years.

Blue whales stay with their mother until they are around 7 months old. Then they are able to stop drinking their mother's milk and start eating things like krill, which is a blue whale favorite.

28

Kangaroos

Kangaroo babies are called joeys, and spend much of their young lives close to their mothers and even riding in a pouch on the mother's belly.

When a joey is outside of the pouch and gets scared by a predator or something else, it will dive back into the pouch head first and then have to rearrange itself so that its head is facing out again.

Mother kangaroo's bodies make different kinds of milk with different kinds of vitamins as the joey ages, so that the joey is always getting exactly what it needs to be healthy.

It's rare, but kangaroo twins do exist, and both joeys will share the pouch at the same time!

Cows

Similar to a human mother, a cow mother is pregnant for around 9 months.

Baby calves are able to stand on their own and even moo only

minutes after being born. This is common for animals like cows, deers, horses, and other herd prey animals because they need to be able to run away from predators and move with their group.

Calves are very social, and will try to spend time with any other calf in the herd and even several different adults. Often these bonds last a lifetime and cows are known to have the same friends their entire life.

<h1 style="text-align:center">30</h1>

Elephants

Just like some young humans suck on their thumbs for comfort, baby elephants will comfort themselves by sucking on their trunks.

Elephants are blind when they are born. Their eyesight slowly develops, but at first they have to rely on their other senses and their parent's help.

Mother elephants cover their babies in sand and dirt to help protect them from the sun. A baby elephant's skin is not as tough against the sun as an adult, so older elephants will use their trunks to gather up sand and dirt and sprinkle the baby elephant with it so that the sun doesn't hit their skin as much.

Giant Anteaters

Unlike most babies, anteaters are very quiet. Except for an occasional squeak while they are eating, they are almost silent.

Anteater mothers cannot pick up their babies with their paws because of their claws, and they cannot pick them up with their mouths because of their long jaws. This means that the baby has to be born knowing how to climb so that whenever the mom is going somewhere it can climb onto her back and go for a ride.

Because giant anteaters are not very social animals, their mother might be the only other anteater a baby meets for the first months or even the first year of its life.

32

Whitetail Deer

Baby deer, called fawns, spend most of the day alone or with other fawns in a hiding spot. The rest of their herd leaves to find food and the mother deer usually checks in on them in the morning and at night.

Fawns can have around 300 white spots that help with camouflage. Some of the spots will go away as they get older and adult whitetail deer do not have nearly as many.

It is most common for them to be born in pairs, as twins. If it is an area with lots of good food and where the mother is very healthy, then she can even have triplets.

33

Bats

B aby bats are called pups, just like dogs, seals, and some other animals!

Bats often live in large groups, called colonies, and the babies love to find each other and all cuddle together in a big crowd. There is often a spot in a bat cave that the whole colony will use as a nursery or preschool, and the babies will all be put there while the adults go hunting.

Baby bats are great at learning how to do something by watching it. When they are big enough they will actually hold on to older bats as they leave the cave so that they can learn how to fly and use echolocation, which is a big part of how bats move around and see the world.

34

Sea Otters

R iver otters are born blind and without teeth, but can hunt for themselves by around 2 months old. Sea otters are born much more developed, but tend to rely on their parents to get enough food for up to 6 months.

A sea otter mother will spend time carrying her pup on her belly as she swims. When she needs to dive to get food she will find an area with a lot of kelp and gently wrap her baby in it so that they don't float away.

Baby sea otters will often sleep on their mother's bellies, and the adults in the group will all hold each other's paws while they sleep to help keep the ocean currents from separating the group while they sleep.

35

Conclusion

I hope you have enjoyed learning something about some of the animals we share the planet with. There are a lot of different kinds of creatures out there, and far more facts to be uncovered. I encourage you to go learn more about your favorite animal, or any animal for that matter! I also encourage you to share some of your favorite facts from this book with your friends and family, or anyone else who loves animals. Lastly, if you liked this book, try to give it a good review on Amazon so that more people might be able to see it and learn more about the cool animals that we just did.

36

Resources

10 Fun Facts About Whitetail Fawns. (2020, June 10). Big Deer Blog. Retrieved August 4, 2022, from https://bigdeerblog.com/2019/06/10-fun-facts-about-whitetail-fawns/

15 AMAZING OCTOPUS FACTS FOR KIDS AND GROW-UPS ALIKE! (2022). Toucanbox. Retrieved August 4, 2022, from https://www.toucanbox.com/facts-for-kids/octopus-facts

Achwal, A. (2020, September 17). Interesting Facts About Goats for Kids. FirstCry Parenting. Retrieved August 4, 2022, from https://parenting.firstcry.com/articles/interesting-facts-about-goat-for-kids/

All About Otters - Birth & Care of Young| SeaWorld Parks & Entertainment. (2022). Seaworld. Retrieved August 4, 2022, from https://seaworld.org/animals/all-about/otters/care-of-young/

Anteater Facts. (2019). Animal Facts Encyclopedia. Retrieved August 4, 2022, from https://www.animalfactsencyclopedia.com

/Anteater-facts.html

Breyer, M. (2021, November 9). 11 Facts About Blue Whales, the Largest Animals Ever on Earth. Treehugger. Retrieved August 4, 2022, from https://www.treehugger.com/facts-about-blue-whal es-largest-animals-ever-known-earth-4858813

Chickens. (2019, April 10). Easy Science For Kids. Retrieved August 4, 2022, from https://easyscienceforkids.com/all-about-chickens/

Colgate. (2019, August 12). How Many Dog Breeds Are There? Hill's Pet Nutrition. Retrieved August 4, 2022, from https://ww w.hillspet.com/dog-care/behavior-appearance/how-many-dog-breeds-are-there

Cool and Interesting Frog Facts for Kids. (2020, April 2). Yowie World. Retrieved August 4, 2022, from https://yowieworld.com/blog/cool-frog-facts/

Cool Kid Facts. (2022a, July 14). Penguin Facts. Retrieved August 4, 2022, from
https://www.coolkidfacts.com/penguin-facts/

Cool Kid Facts. (2022b, July 15). Fun Hamster Facts for Kids. Retrieved August 4, 2022, from https://www.coolkidfacts.com/hamster-facts-for-kids/

Cool Kid Facts. (2022c, July 15). Interesting Fun Horse Facts for Kids [Pictures Inside]. Retrieved August 4, 2022, from https://ww w.coolkidfacts.com/horse-facts/

Cosgrove, N. (2022, July 28). 36 Fascinating & Fun Rabbit Facts You Never Knew. Pet Keen. Retrieved August 4, 2022, from https://pe tkeen.com/rabbit-facts/

D. (2022, April 11). Cat Facts for Kids. Facts Just for Parents, Teachers and Students. Retrieved August 4, 2022, from https://w ww.factsjustforkids.com/animal-facts/cat-facts-for-kids/

Duffy, J. (2018, September 11). 5 Kangaroo Joey Facts You've Never Heard Before. Echidna Walkabout Tours. Retrieved August 4, 2022, from https://www.echidnawalkabout.com.au/kangaroo-j oey-facts/

Dunlap, S. (2021a, December 4). What's a Baby Elephant Called & 9 More Amazing Facts! AZ Animals. Retrieved August 4, 2022, from https://a-z-animals.com/blog/baby-elephants-9-facts-and -pictures/

Dunlap, S. (2021b, December 27). Baby Bat: 5 Pictures & 5 Facts. AZ Animals. Retrieved August 4, 2022, from https://a-z-animals. com/blog/baby-bat-five-facts-five-pictures/

Fun Flamingo Facts for Kids - Interesting Information about Flamingos. (2020). Sciencekids. Retrieved August 4, 2022, from https://www.sciencekids.co.nz/sciencefacts/animals/flamingo. html

Fun Guinea Pig Facts for Kids - Interesting Information about Guinea Pigs. (2020). Sciencekids. Retrieved August 4, 2022, from https://www.sciencekids.co.nz/sciencefacts/animals/guineapig. html

Fun Parrot Facts for Kids - Interesting Information about Parrots. (2022). Sciencekids. Retrieved August 4, 2022, from https://www.sciencekids.co.nz/sciencefacts/animals/parrot.html

Guinea Pig - Animal Facts for Kids - Characteristics & Pictures. (2022). Animalfunfacts. Retrieved August 4, 2022, from https://www.animalfunfacts.net/rodents/114-guinea-pig.html

Jones, A. (2021, July 18). Goldfish Facts: 20 Mind-blowing Goldfish Facts! The Goldfish Tank. Retrieved August 4, 2022, from https://thegoldfishtank.com/goldfish-facts/

Kane, P. (2022, June 23). Killer whale facts for kids. National Geographic Kids. Retrieved August 4, 2022, from https://www.natgeokids.com/uk/discover/animals/sea-life/killer-whale-facts/

Lever, A. (2022, March 21). Dog facts for kids! National Geographic Kids. Retrieved August 4, 2022, from https://www.natgeokids.com/uk/discover/animals/general-animals/dog-facts/

Lines, A. (2022, July 18). 30+ Pigs Facts For Kids: Learn All About The Smartest Farmyard Animal. PetKeen. Retrieved August 4, 2022, from https://kidadl.com/education-learning/pigs-facts-for-kids-learn-all-about-the-smartest-farmyard-animal

Science, E. (2018, August 27). Chimpanzees – The Most intelligent Animals on Earth. Easy Science For Kids. Retrieved August 4, 2022, from https://easyscienceforkids.com/all-about-chimpanzees/

Sidder, A. (2022). Black Bear. National Geographic. Retrieved

August 4, 2022, from https://kids.nationalgeographic.com/anim als/mammals/facts/black-bear

Team, K. H. Q. (2021a, February 16). Cow Facts. KonnectHQ. Retrieved August 4, 2022, from https://www.konnecthq.com/ cow-facts/

Team, K. H. Q. (2021b, April 30). Raccoon Facts. KonnectHQ. Retrieved August 4, 2022, from https://www.konnecthq.com/ raccoon-facts/

Team, K. H. Q. (2021c, June 21). Wolf Facts. KonnectHQ. Retrieved August 4, 2022, from https://www.konnecthq.com/wolf-facts/

Top 10 Facts About Giraffes. (2021, December 9). Fun Kids - the UK's Children's Radio Station. Retrieved August 4, 2022, from https://www.funkidslive.com/learn/top-10-facts/top-10-giraff e-facts/

U.S. pet ownership statistics. (2022). American Veterinary Medical Association. Retrieved August 4, 2022, from https://www .avma.org/resources-tools/reports-statistics/us-pet-ownership- statistics

www.ingramcontent.com/pod-product-compliance
Lightning Source LLC
Chambersburg PA
CBHW072120150726
47999CB00005B/2050